The Real Gh
Gut-busting

Jonathan Clements

CARNIVAL

Carnival
An imprint of the Children's Division
of the Collins Publishing Group
8 Grafton Street, London W1X 3LA

Published by Carnival 1989

ISBN 0 00 194634 X

Printed and bound in Glasgow by
Collins, Glasgow.

Set in Times.

THE REAL GHOSTBUSTERS™

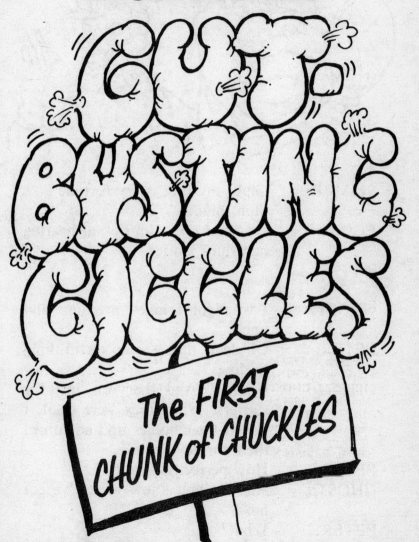

GUT-BUSTING GIGGLES

The FIRST CHUNK of CHUCKLES

| SLIMER: | Glub, my face is my fortune . . . blub, blub. |
| EGON: | Oh, shut up – I'm sick of hearing hard-luck stories. |

GHOST:	Last night I killed my aunt and uncle.
PETER:	Oh dear, that was an awful thing to do.
GHOST:	I know. And that was just for starters. When they were dead, I boiled their bodies up and forced them through a sieve.
PETER:	How perfectly dreadful!
GHOST:	And do you know what I've got now?
PETER:	What?
GHOST:	Strained relations.

JANINE:	I think you're so *brave*, Peter.
PETER:	Aw shucks, thanks.
JANINE:	That's all right. I mean, with a face like yours, I wouldn't ever dare set foot outside of the house.

PETER:	I'm off to Africa to catch a killer ghost.
JANINE:	Byeeee! Don't forget to drop us a lion!

RAY:	Hey, Egon, what do ghoulies and vampires hate having for dinner?
EGON:	I dunno – what?
RAY:	T-Bone stakes.

GURU:	I have been pondering for ten years about my belief in Buddha.
PETER:	And what are your conclusions, O Wise One?
GURU:	Well, I still think there's a lot to be said in favour of margarine.

LIMP-ALONG:	Hey, Mr Ghost, how much would you charge to haunt my dread rival, Perry Palooka?
GHOST:	For just £20, I'll scare him out of his wits.
LIMP-ALONG:	Here's £10. He's only a half-wit.

EGON:	What do you think of Beethoven's Fifth?
RAY:	A lovely girl.

WINSTON: Why didn't the ghoul do the football pools?

PETER: He didn't think he had the ghost of a chance of winning.

RAY: I was thinking of having my fortune told, Egon. Which do you think would be best – a palmist or a mind-reader.

EGON: A palmist.

RAY: Why's that?

EGON: At least you know you've got a palm.

PETER:	When I was in Africa, I went out hunting a man-eating tiger with just a club.
RAY:	Only a *club*? Gosh, Pete, I never knew you were so brave. Weren't you scared at all?
PETER:	Shucks, no. After all, there were about two hundred members in the club.

EGON:	I know this ghost that makes a new Will & Testament every week.
JANINE:	Why does he do that?
EGON:	I guess he's nothin' but a fresh heir fiend.

PETER:	There's talk around town, Slimer, that a big producer is interested in making a movie out of your life story.
SLIMER:	Glub, glug, really?
PETER:	Yeah – he reckons it will make a really great horror film!

EGON:	We've got a grandfather clock that's been in the family for over two hundred years.
JANINE (yawning):	How incredibly fascinating.
EGON:	Hey, don't mock the clock! We raised it from a tiny little wrist watch.

A man whose house was over-run with ghosts and ghouls and green dripping things phoned The Ghostbusters and cried: 'Hurry, hurry – come over and get rid of these ghastly things in my house!'

'Certainly, sir,' said Egon, trying to calm down the hysterical man. 'Now – how do we get to your house?'

'What!' shouted the man. 'Haven't you still got your customised, supercharged Ecto-1 ghost mobile?'

DOCTOR: Breathe out five times.
RAY: Is this to test my lungs, Doc?
DOCTOR: No, it's just that my glasses need cleaning.

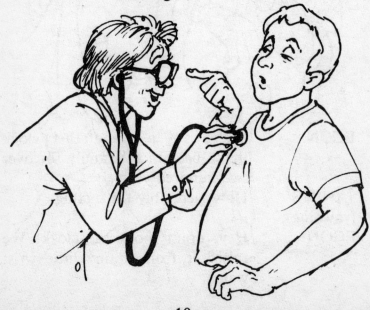

RAY:	I've just had an idea, and I think it's a good one.
PETER:	Beginner's luck!

PETER:	I'm glad I'm not a bird. I might get killed.
JANINE:	Why?
PETER:	I can't fly?

WINSTON:	Hey, Peter, look at those two girls. Do you think they're identical twins?
PETER:	No; they both go to the same plastic surgeon.

JANINE:	Do you believe the old saying that you get seven years bad luck if you break a mirror?
WINSTON:	Naaaah – that's just an old wive's tale. My brother Norm broke a mirror, and he never had seven years bad luck.
JANINE:	He didn't?
WINSTON:	Of course not. Mind you, he was killed by an explosion the same day.

BABY GHOST:	Boooo--hoooo! Boooo--hoooo!
WINSTON:	Hey, little ghost, why are you crying?
BABY GHOST:	Because you rotten Ghostbusters have just killed my Dad and my Mum.
WINSTON:	We're awfully sorry, kid, but we had to. Did you love them very much!
BABY GHOST:	No, I hated them. But can you guess who's got to dig their graves?

RAY:	One thing has always puzzled me – where *do* all the bugs go in winter-time?
SLIMER:	Gloop, doop. Search me.
RAY:	No thanks. I was just wondering.

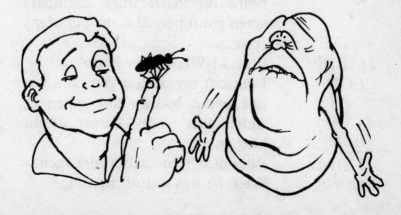

PETER: This hamburger you made has a peculiar taste, Janine.

JANINE: That's funny; it should be OK. I did burn it a little bit, but I put lots of antiseptic cream and a bandage on it.

EGON: I was just about to make some beans on toast, when a slithery green ghost peered at me out of my cooker.

JANINE: Eeeeek! What did you do?

EGON: I got out my proton gun, and was just about to zap him when he flitted over to the corner of the kitchen.

JANINE: Why didn't you shoot him then?

EGON: Well, he was out of my range.

How does the Abominable Snowman travel?
Bi-Icicle.

What's the best way to buy holes?
Wholesale.

What do you call a large group of protesting demons and ghouls?
A demon-stration.

What's the best way to make an ice-cream stand?
Steal its chair.

Why are ghosts very simple creatures?
Because they can easily be seen through.

What is the most important thing to be if you want to be a ghost?
Dead.

How do scarecrows greet each other?
'Hay, man!'

What did Egon say to the kid ghost when he got it into his car?
'Fasten your sheet-belt.'

What did the weak ghost say to the bully ghoul?
'Leave me alone or I'll tell my Mummy!'

How do ghosts like their eggs?
Terror-fried.

What do ghosts like best for dinner?
Ghoul–lash.

What's the difference between a girl and a postage stamp?
One is a female and the other is a male-fee.

What did the first long-dead Ghoul say to the second long-dead Ghoul when they parted company?
'B.C.-ing you!'

Why did the paper doll look crummy in shorts?
Because she wasn't cut out for them.

How does an electric rabbit greet you?
'Watts up, Doc?'

How does a fiend welcome you to a crypt?
'Hello there; let me shake you by the throat . . . .'

When is it considered good manners to spit in a man's face?
When his moustache is on fire.

What did Slimer call his bride-to-be?
His ghoul-friend.

What is the soft, mushy stuff between a shark's teeth?
Slow swimmers.

18

Why did the pop music fan hold a stone up to her left ear and a hamburger bun up to her right ear?
Because she wanted to hear some rock and roll.

What did the chewing gum say to the shoe?
'Hey-I'm really stuck on you.'

How does one dinosaur tell another to hurry up?
'Pronto, Saurus!'

How did the firefly feel when he ran into a fan?
De-lighted.

What did the ground say to the rain?
'If you keep that up, my name will be mud.'

What game do little ghosts like to play?
Corpse and Robbers.

What flowers do ghosts like growing?
Marighouls and Mourning-Gorys.

What's wrong with letting a smile be your umbrella?
You wind up with very wet teeth.

What happens if a burglar falls into a cement mixer?
He comes out a hardened criminal.

What did the motorway say to the slip-road?
'Did you ever get that run-down feeling?'

What do you get if you tear a neck-scarf in two?
A bandana-split.

Why is it very hard to drive a golf ball?
Because it doesn't have a steering wheel.

What happened when the boy and girl tried to kiss in a dense fog?
They missed.

Where do hikers keep their sleeping pills?
In their nap-sacks.

Why is a billiard hall a good place to go when you don't feel well?
Because you will come across some brilliant cue-rs.

How do you send a message to a Viking?
By Norse-Code.

Why can't a bicycle stand by itself?
Because it's two-tyred.

How did Anthony meet Cleopatra on the Nile?
He just barged in.

What kind of monkey eats chips?
A chipmunk.

Why did the cowboy die with his boots on?
He didn't want to stub his toe when he kicked the bucket.

If you are ever locked out, what should you do?
Keep singing songs till you find one with the right key.

Where do geologists go for relaxation?
To rock concerts.

What do you call a carpenter who loses his tools?
A saw loser.

What do canaries say at Halloween?
'Twick or tweet!'

What do you call a person who chucks rubbish at families of cats?
A litter-lout.

What's the best way to paint a rabbit?
With hare-spray.

THE REAL GHOSTBUSTERS™

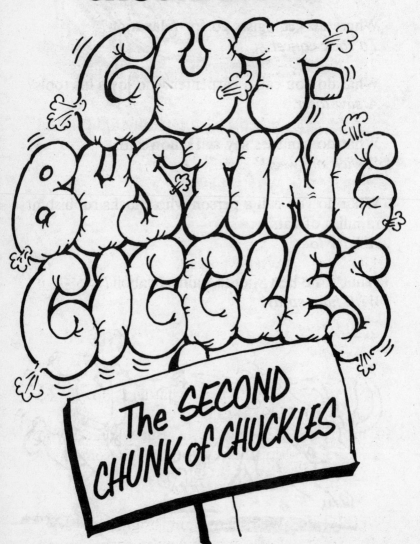

The SECOND CHUNK of CHUCKLES

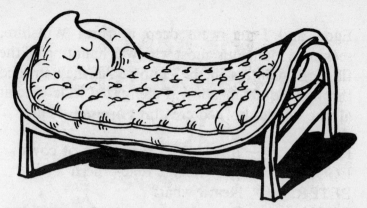

1ST GHOST:	When I died, I really didn't want to come back as a ghost.
2ND GHOST:	Why's that?
1ST GHOST:	I wanted to come back as a mattress.
2ND GHOST:	Whatever for?
1ST GHOST:	So I could lie around on a bed all day!

| WINSTON (Driving Ecto-1 at 100 mph): | Hey, Pete, what'll I do if the brakes fail? |
| PETER: | I dunno . . . . But whatever you do, make sure you hit something *cheap*! |

| PETER: | Well, here I am, bright and early! |
| WINSTON: | Let's just say you're early. |

Egon and Peter were deep in rural Wiltshire, seeking a malicious ghost who was haunting all the flagpole painters in the county. As they strolled through a quiet meadow, Peter gazed wide-eyed at all the docile, horned creatures around them.

PETER: Just look at that flock of cows.

EGON: Not 'flock', Pete– 'herd'.

PETER: Heard what?

EGON: Of cows.

PETER: Of course I've heard of cows.

EGON: No, I mean a *cow herd*.

PETER: I don't care. I have no secrets from them!

EGON: My great-great grandfather fought against the Boers; my grandfather saw action in the First World War, and my uncle fought against the Germans in World War 2.

RAY: Good grief, Egon, couldn't your family get along with *anybody*?

JANINE: Oh, nobody understands me! I'm a warm, emotional person at heart. I want to be squeezed; I want to be hugged; I want to be held tight! What shall I do?

PETER: Buy a whalebone corset.

| JUDGE: | Order in court! |
| PETER: | A corned-beef sandwich and a Cola, please. |

1ST GOBLIN:	Last night I had that young couple who moved in down the road over for dinner at my place.
2ND GOBLIN:	Really? And what were they like?
1ST GOBLIN:	Delicious!

WINSTON:	Didn't that ghost swear terribly?
PETER:	He certainly did. He just didn't put *any* expression into the words at all.

RAY:	What was that terrible noise just now?
EGON:	Oh, it was just Revolting Rita the gruesome goblin, falling down a flight of stairs, trying to escape.
RAY:	Cellar?
EGON:	No, who'd buy her? We might as well sling her in the containment unit, like the others.

PETER:	I hear you're becoming quite famous, Slimer.
SLIMER:	Glub . . . glug . . . yeah?
PETER:	Well, a big costume company is using your face as a model for a Hallowe'en mask!

EGON: I hear that eating fish improves
            one's brain.
JANINE: Sure. I eat fish all of the time
EGON: Oh well, another theory bites the
            dust.

A long time ago, Egon went through a craze on
wanting to be a famous pop singer. He took
lessons on how not to sing; formed a group called
the Rollin' Ratfinks, and even got an agent named
Tina Delight.

But gigs were hard to get for the Ratfinks. One
day, Egon had a phone call from his agent, who
said: 'I'm awfully sorry about this, Egon. It's a
very difficult time on the music scene, and I'm
terribly upset that I haven't been able to get more
jobs for you and the band . . .'

'Ah, that's all right, I understand,' said Egon.
'Please don't cry for me, agent Tina . . .'

SLIMER:	Gloop, bloop, glub. Do you think I've got bad breath, Ray?
RAY:	Well, you're the only . . . thing I know who eats garlic to improve it.
SLIMER:	Oh . . . Glob, blob. But I can be a charmer, eh?
RAY:	Sure. All that's stopping you is your hideous looks, your evil ways and your truly horrendous personality.

JANINE:	Winston doesn't look very well today, Peter.
PETER:	I know. I've just given him a brief examination; he doesn't seem to have a fever or anything.
JANINE:	Did you take his temperature?
PETER:	Why – is it missing?

PETER: I'd like to buy my girlfriend Myrtle
            a present. What do you think she'd
            like?
EGON: Well . . . does she like you?
PETER: Of course she does.
EGON: Then it should be easy, Peter. If
            she likes you, she'll like *anything*!

RAY: My grandfather Moses used to be
            with a ghost circus. He was a
            zombie-trainer.
WINSTON: Oh. And how did he treat the
            zombies?
RAY: With the utmost respect.

JANINE: What's the best way to stop a man-eating ghost from charging?

EGON: Just take away his credit cards.

WINSTON: Did you know that King Arthur's castle in Tintagel was haunted by the ghosts of dead werewolves and sorcerers?

RAY: No, I didn't.

WINSTON: Yes. It must have been awful. On one occasion, King Arthur and fifty of his men were held at seige for over a month, while they fought a bloody battle with the ghosts and demons. Not a moment's rest did they get in all that time.

RAY: Wow! Now that's what I call a lot of sleepless knights . . . .

BOY GHOST: Aw, Dad – I want to go out and get into houses and make funny noises and hideous faces and scare the living daylights out of people.

DAD GHOST: Now, now, lad. Wait your turn. Don't spook until you're spooken to.

PETER:	I just knew I'd be unlucky on this case. We had dinner on the train, and there were thirteen people at the table.
EGON:	What makes you think that thirteen people at the table was unlucky?
PETER:	*I* had to pay the bill!

Peter arrived at Ghostbusters HQ an hour late for a special meeting of The Ghostbusters. His clothes were hanging in tatters; his head was bandaged and he was bruised and cut in several places.

'This meeting was supposed to begin at 10 o'clock,' snapped Janine. 'Where have you been?'

'I'm sorry I'm late,' groaned Peter. 'But I fell out of a ten-storey window.'

'And that took you a whole *hour* . . . .?'

EGON:	To be a doughnut or not to be a doughnut, that is the question.
RAY:	Aren't you getting food mixed up with Shakespeare?
EGON:	Yes, but then I've just drunk two pints of lemonade.
RAY:	What's that got to do with it?
EGON:	Two pints make a quote, don't they?

WINSTON: We'd better do something quick to change the status quo.

PETER: What's 'status quo'?

WINSTON: It's Latin for 'The awful mess we're in'.

PETER: Last night, Slimer, I dreamed I saw something in front of HQ that made me very happy.

SLIMER: Gloop, doop. What?

PETER: A removals van, with your name on it.

EGON: What would you like first – the
           good news or the bad news?
RAY: The good news.
EGON: The good news is that the family of
           headless ghouls are moving out of
           the haunted house next door.
RAY: And what's the bad news?
EGON: The ghouls are only going because
           a tribe of man-eating zombies
           from outer-space are moving in.

Janine's LOOPY LIMERICKS

Having made a remark rather coarse,
Peter was seized with remorse;
He fled from the group,
And later, a snoop
Saw him chasing a ghost on a horse.

Dear Winston, otherwise meek,
Detested with passion the leek:
When offered one out,
He dealt such a clout,
To the cook, she was out for a week.

The Ghostbusters, in a house quite charmless,
Was informed its ghoul was quite harmless:
'If you're caught unawares,
At the top of the stairs,
Don't panic-he's eyeless and armless.'

Janine, feeling callous and brash,
Met a man with a vast black moustache.
She cried 'Oh, shave it do!
And I'll fix it with glue,
To my hat, as a sort of panache.'

Slimer was once seized with intent,
To revise his existence mis-spent.
So he climbed up the dome,
Of St Peter's in Rome,
Where he stayed through the following Lent.

When Winston lived by the Usk,
He existed each day on a rusk.
He ate the first bite,
Before it was light,
And the last crumb some time after dusk.

To a weepy young woman in Thrums,
Egon remarked 'This is what comes
Of allowing your tears
To fall into my ears—
I think they have rotted the drums.'

An innocent maiden named Garage,
Was cruelly tricked into marriage;
When she later found out
What her spouse was about,
She threw herself under a carriage.

Ray grew increasingly peaky,
In a house where the hinges were squeaky:
The ferns curled up brown,
The ceilings fell down,
And all of the taps, they were leaky.

Long ago, young Peter appeared,
To his friends, with a knee-length beard;
When they all hollered 'Shave!'
He just wouldn't behave;
So they put him with the sheep to be sheared.

There was a weird ghost whose brain,
Was deranged from drinking champagne;
He lured a small chair
To his subterranean lair,
Where he beat it to death with his cane.

Young Frankenstein, for spilling his soup,
Was put out for the night on the stoop;
In the morning he'd not,
Repented a jot;
The next day he was dead of the croup.

An old gentleman's crotchets and quibblings,
Were a terrible trial to his siblings,
But he was not removed,
Till one day it was proved,
The dustbin was damp with his dribblings.

From Number Ten, Pilkington Mews,
There is really abominable news:
They've discovered a head,
In the box for the bread,
And nobody seems to know whose . . .

THE REAL GHOSTBUSTERS™

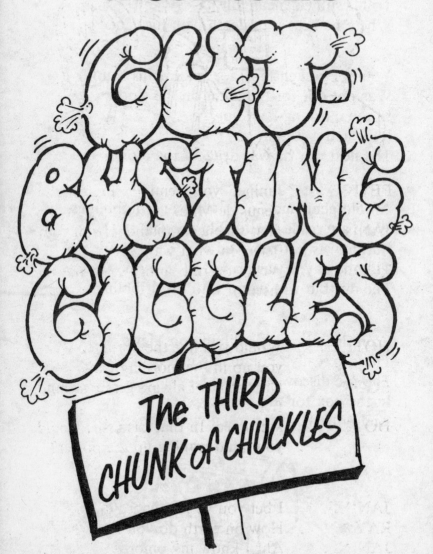

GUT-BUSTING GIGGLES

The THIRD CHUNK of CHUCKLES

PETER: Janine, you remind me of the Venus de Milo.

JANINE: That's a big compliment from you, Peter. In what way?

PETER: Well, you're beautiful, but not all there.

HOTELIER: Would you like the porter to wake you up in the morning, sir?

EGON: No, thanks. I always get up around five.

HOTELIER: Ah, I see. In that case, sir, would you mind waking up the porter?

JANINE: I bet you've just had dinner.

RAY: How on earth do you know?

JANINE: Ah, I know my onions!

WINSTON:	I say, can you tell me how far it is to the village of Lower Desolation?
LOCAL:	Arrr. As you're headed, about 35,000 miles.
WINSTON:	But that's ridiculous! I saw it on a signpost about five or so miles back.
LOCAL:	Arrr, then you've gone right past it. Turn around; it's only about two miles.

JANINE:	What breed of dog is that mutt you've got there, Winston?
WINSTON:	It's a bloodhound.
JANINE:	Doesn't look much like a bloodhound to me.
WINSTON:	A fat lot you know. I'll prove it to you. Hey, Bonzo – bleed for the lady . . .

1ST GHOST:	Booooooo! Woooooooo! Owwww! Hoooooooowl!
2ND GHOST:	Zjhh! Mzzzzzzzzzzyh! Onnnnnnjxch! Snnnnnnnkyk!
1ST GHOST:	What on earth are you on about? We ghosts don't talk like that.
2ND GHOST:	If you don't mind, mush, I'm trying to learn a foreign language.

PETER:	Hey, Isobel, let's run away to Tahiti together!
ISOBEL:	What?
PETER:	You heard. Just imagine it; life in Tahiti; lying around on the warm beaches all day, eating doughnuts.
ISOBEL:	Certainly not, Peter. And if that's the kind of stupid layabout you are, I'm breaking off our engagement. My feelings towards you have changed.
PETER:	Oh, very well. If that's how you feel, may I have my engagement ring back?
ISOBEL:	No. My feelings towards you might have changed, but I still feel the same about the ring.

45

| SLIMER: | Grump, hump. I'm so *bored*. |
| PETER: | I know the cure for that, Slimer. Get a job as a dustman and lose yourself in your work. |

RAY:	Last night I dreamed about horse racing. In my dream I had a bet on the eighth race, on a horse called 'Eight Angels'. So this afternoon I put £8 on it to win at 8-1.
EGON:	And did it win?
RAY:	No. It came in eighth.

RAY:	Truth is beauty.
EGON:	Are you positive?
RAY:	Only fools are positive.
EGON:	Are you quite sure about that?
RAY:	I'm positive.

PETER: Is it true you were offered the position as President of The League of Ghostbusters?

WINSTON: That's right. But I turned it down.

PETER: Why?

WINSTON: In a job like that, there's no room for advancement!

WINSTON: Is Professor Peabody of the University for Supernatural Phenomenon one of those absent-minded professors?

PETER: I'll say he is. Once, he hid his face in his hands, and it was a week before he found it!

After a long chase, The Ghostbusters had cornered the dangerous ghost named Shriek in a corner of a deserted warehouse.

'OK Shriek!' commanded Egon. 'We've got you surrounded. Make it easy on yourself and come out with your hands up.'

All The Ghostbusters raised their proton guns as the fiendish shape flickered into view. They fired at him and caught him in the cross beams of their proton guns.

'You've been really dreadful,' said Egon. 'You've frightened over fifty people to death with your sick hauntings; you've caused the destruction of property worth millions; your library books are a month overdue; and you've raised from the dead some of the worst villains in history to help you with your ghastly schemes. Well, what have you got to say for yourself?'

'Gee whizz, boss,' mumbled Shriek. 'Nobody's *perfect*!'

WINSTON: You've sure got a big mouth, Janine.

JANINE: What are you inferring, lump head?

WINSTON: Well, you're the only person I know who can eat a banana sideways.

JANINE: Huh!

WINSTON: Furthermore, you are often heard singing duets with yourself . . .

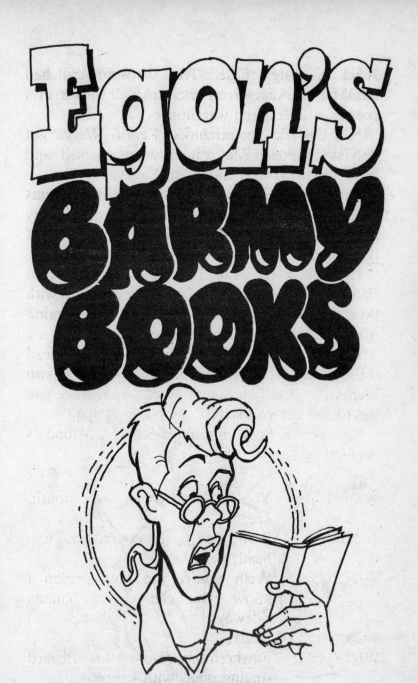

'THE WONDER CURE-ALL' by Penny Sillun
'HOME-HEATING MADE EASY' by Ray D. Aytor
'RICE CROPS IN CHINA' by Paddy Fields
'I NEVER WASH' by Phil T. Hans
'REPTILES OF AFRICA' by Sal A. Mander
'FROM TOOTING TO TOKYO' by Miles Apart
'MAD MUSIC' by Clare de Loon
'GUNFIGHTERS OF THE WEST' by Rick O'Shea
'VIOLENCE IN THE INNER CITIES' by Ed Banging
'MY LIFE WITH MOP & PAIL' by Lew Kleener
'COSMETIC TIPS' by I. Liner
'INTOLERABLE BURDENS' by Cy Heavily
'MAKING LOUD EXPLOSIONS' by Dinah Might
'SAFER SUNBATHING' by Nat Repellant

'WHAT IS THE ANSWER?' by Howard I. Noe
'IT WASN'T HOT & IT WASN'T COLD' by
Luke Warm
'THE PSYCHOLOGY OF PAIN AND
by Ann Gwish
'AEROBICS FOR ALL' by Ben Dover
'EVERYONE CAN HELP' by Linda Hand
'WILL HE WIN?' by Betty Wont
'RESTORING OLD FURNITURE' by Ann Teak
'CURING TROPICAL DISEASES' by I.
Scratchem
'CLASSICAL BALLET DANCING' by Tippy
Toe
'KIDNAPPING MADE EASY' by Caeser Quick
'I SWAM AROUND FINLAND' by I. C. Waters
'MY LIFE AS A MIDGET' by Ammonia Littlun
'CAKES AND PASTRIES' by Mac O'Roon
'HOW TO BE TALLER' by R. U. Stunted
'HAVE I GOT PROBLEMS!' by Mona Lott
'MATHEMATICS' by Adam Uppe
'SECRETS OF TUG-OF-WAR' by Eve Mightilee
'ONE-WHEELED CYCLES' Una Pod
'NATURE'S MAGIC PLANTS' by Herb Garden
'20 YEARS IN OPERA' by Topsy Hitter
'CONQUERING DEAFNESS' by Isobel Ringing
'SMOKING IS BAD FOR YOU' by Nick O'Teen
'A HISTORY OF LIGHTHOUSES' by Eddie
Stone
'SPACE WEAPONS' by Rae Gunn
'EASTERN COOKING' by Ali Carte

'WHY THINGS GO WRONG' by Major Setbacks
'A HISTORY OF CARS' by Otto Mobeel
'AT THE SOUTH POLE' by Anne Tartick
'LEARNING MAGIC' by Beatrix Ster
'HELPING THE UNDERPRIVILEGED' by Ada Charitee

'A MIGHTY CLOSE SHAVE' by Ray Zurr
'THE DECLINE OF ETIQUETTE' by Kurt B. Havier
'STARTING ALL OVER AGAIN' by Donovan U. Era
'THE COLD AND THE FLU' by Carmen Aylements
'I'LL BE THERE SOON' by Isa Cumming

THE REAL GHOSTBUSTERS™

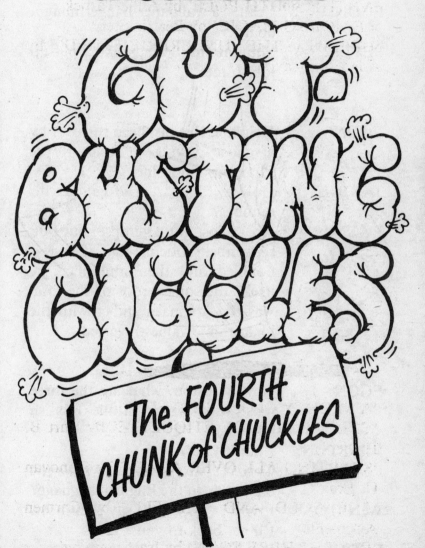

GUT-BUSTING GIGGLES

The FOURTH CHUNK of CHUCKLES

EGON: There's been a terrible murder at No 42 Ectoplasm Mews.

PETER: Really?

EGON: Yeah – a wallpaper-hanger hung a boarder.

PETER: Mmmmmm. Sounds like a put-up job to me.

EGON: Help me. I've just been run over by a ghost driving a Rolls Royce Phantom limousine.

JANINE: How awful . . . . Did you get his number?

EGON: No – I just got a glimpse, but I do remember noticing that if it was doubled and then multiplied by itself, the square root of the total was the original number with the logarithmic values reversed.

EGON: Hey, Winston, what are the three most used words in the English language?

WINSTON: I don't know.

EGON: Correct. Next question: what's the biggest lie in the English language?

WINSTON: Errrrr . . . . I can't say right now. I'll get back to you.

EGON: Right again!

SLIMER: I just happen to be a natural horseman.

EGON: Oh yeah?

SLIMER: Yes; people often tell me that when I'm in the saddle, I become part of the horse.

EGON: Yes, but do they tell you *which* part?

PETER: Is Janine a good bridge player?

WINSTON: No, she's terrible. The last time we played, I couldn't tell by the expressions she gave me how she would play.

PETER: Oh, poker-face?

WINSTON: No, but I wanted to.

Whilst helping the other Ghostbusters chase an elusive evil spirit through the jungles of Borneo, Peter got bitten by a deadly-looking snake. Within minutes he collapsed, and went as white as a sheet. The others picked him up, and anxiously carried him as quickly as they could to the nearest village.

'We've got a sick man here,' Egon told one of the natives. 'Is there a doctor in the village?'

'Only Momboola, the witch-doctor.'

'He'll have to do. Hurry and take us to him.'

They made their way to the witch-doctor's hut, and the weird-looking Momboola examined Peter for a long time. He turned to the Ghostbusters and said: 'Your friend is in a bad way. I will make up a special magicial potion for him. The potion will contain ground lizard tail; alligator knee; toad's tongue; yak kidney; hair from a left-footed rhinoceros and a secret elixir from the sacred Lake Ooooji. He must drink this potion in one go at midnight.'

'What if it doesn't work?' asked Winston.

'In that case,' smiled Momboola. 'Give him two aspirins every four hours.'

EGON: That's quite a Cabinet the Prime Minister has, isn't it?

WINSTON: It sure is.

EGON: If you ask me, they ought to lock it up and throw away the key!

JANINE: My Aunt Mabel had her face lifted.

RAY: Oh? How did they do it?

JANINE: With a piece of rope around her neck.

EGON: What was that ghost doing at the funfair?

PETER: Oh, he just wanted a ride on the roller-ghoster.

EGON: There's one thing I'll say about you, Peter. You're versatile.

PETER: Why thanks, Egon.

EGON: Yep. You can make a mess of *anything*.

PETER: Oh, Isobel, I promise I'll be true and constant to you, my love, as constant as that spreading tree above us, if only you'll say you love—

ISOBEL: Errr, Pete?

PETER: Yes, beloved, what is it?

ISOBEL: That tree happens to be a slippery elm . . .

GRISLY
GHOUL: I've had enough. I surrender. I'm going to kill myself. Where's the best place to shoot myself?

WINSTON: Shoot yourself in the chest. You're dead from the neck up, anyway.

SLIMER: Yubble, gubble, gloop. You don't think I'm a repulsive, sickening, hideous, brainless, dumb cretin with the charm of an old soap dish, do you, Pete?

PETER: Of course I don't, Slimer. But then, what is my opinion against thousands of others?

RAY: My brother Elijah is a pan-handler.

EGON: Oh, yes. Does he work out in the Wild West?

RAY: No; he's an orderly in the local hospital.

JANINE: Are *all* cricketers superstitious?

PETER: Sure they are. Look at me – I make it a rule always to touch the crease with my bat every time I score a run.

WINDOW
CLEANER: Oy! You – why did you kick over my pail of water just now?

PETER: Oh, I was just idly wondering what it felt like to kick the bucket.

PETER: I've just written a book. It's got everything – drama, high comedy, adventure, warmth, wit, suspense and a sparky kind of up-and-at-'em energy.

WINSTON: Sounds pretty good.

PETER: Good – it's brilliant, a message of hope for all mankind. Best of all, the book's main character is truly a great man, somebody who will live forever in the hearts of all mankind the entire world over.

WINSTON: Well, Peter, I can't wait to read your novel-

PETER: *Novel*! What do you mean, novel. This happens to be my *autobiography* . . .

RAY: How are you getting on with Lolita Merryacres?

EGON: I don't think I'm making any progress at all.

RAY: What makes you think that?

EGON: Last night I asked her if I could see her home – and she gave me a picture of it!

RAY: I heard tell that Egon kissed you last night.

JANINE: He *didn't*! Besides, he promised not to tell.

RAY:	All that I am I owe to my mother.
PETER:	Why not send her fifty pence and settle the account?

JANINE:	How are things between you and your girlfriend Isobel lately?
PETER:	Oh, we've split up. Ever since the night I serenaded her under the balcony.
JANINE:	But that was a beautiful, romantic thing to do.
PETER:	The usherette didn't think so.

WINSTON:	How did you get on in that boxing match, Ray?
RAY:	Oh, I lost. I blame it on those big boxing gloves; they always cramp my style.
WINSTON:	How do you mean?
RAY:	Well, have you ever tried to gouge out somebody's eyes or pull their hair wearing those big gloves?

WINSTON:	What's happened around here? Everybody's gone!
JANINE:	Yes, the others were in a great hurry and they left without you. Do I make myself plain?
WINSTON:	No, Janine. God did that.

1ST GHOUL:	What did you do when your wife turned into a pillar of salt?
2ND GHOUL:	Oh, I just put her in the cellar.
1ST FIEND:	Are you coming to my party?
2ND FIEND:	Where are you having it?
1ST FIEND:	In the morgue.
2ND FIEND:	Oh well, the morgue, the merrier!
PETER:	A werewolf bit me on the leg at last night's haunting.
JANINE:	Oh dear. Did you put anything on it?
PETER:	Nope. It must have tasted okay as it was.
EGON:	Do you know 'The St. Louis Blues'?
MUSICIAN:	No, but I know the Browns from Purley.
EGON:	Like a can of cola, Ray?
RAY:	No thanks, Egon. I won't drink anything like that, because I'm afraid of losing my mind.
EGON:	Look, don't worry about it, Ray. How can you lose what you haven't got?

Peter's Delirious Dictionary

A

ABUNDANCE:	A disco for cakes.
ACORN:	Painful little lump caused by a tight shoe.
ANNOUNCE:	One-sixteenth of a pound.
ANTELOPE:	Two ants running away to get married.
ARMIES:	Those long things you have up your sleevies.
ASTRONAUT:	Somebody who's bound to go up in the world.
AUCTIONEER:	A person who looks forbidden.

B

BACTERIA:	The rear entrance of a cafeteria.
BARBER SHOP:	A clip-joint.
BARBEQUE:	A long line of people waiting for a haircut.
BELLY DANCER:	A waist of energy.
BIG GAME HUNTER:	A fan who has lost his way to a football match.
BOROUGH SURVEYOR:	A person who inspects holes dug by rabbits.
BOXING RING:	A punch-bowl.
BUDGET:	A baby budgerigar.

C

CATAS-TROPHE A prize awarded at a cat show.

CEMETERY: Where people who are run down wind up.

COINCIDE: What to do when it's raining.

CONCEIT: 'I' strain.

CORONER: A profession for which you have to take a very stiff examination.

CRANE: A bird who can lift very heavy weights.

CROWBAR: Where big black birds go to get drunk.

D

DIPLOMAT: A person who thinks for a long time before saying nothing.

DISCONSO-LATE: A pop record played loud after midnight.

DIVINE: Where de grapes grow.

DOLDRUMS: Percussion instrument for girls.

E

EARWIG:	False hair for ears.
EGG:	A bird's home town.
ELECTRICIAN:	A switch-doctor.
EVE:	What you do in a tug-of-war contest.
EVEREST:	A really lazy mountain.
EXPERT:	Somebody who used to be pert.

F

FASTIDIOUS:	A ghost who is very ugly and very quick.
FIREMAN:	A person who is always being told, 'Go to blazes!'

G

GARGOYLE:	A mouthwash for monsters.
GHOST-WRITER:	An official spooksman.
GOLF COURSE:	A site to be holed.
GOSSIP:	Somebody who has a great sense of rumour.
GRANARY:	A home for grannies.
GRATEFUL:	A fireplace filled with coal.
GUTTA-PERCHA:	A cat burglar.

H

HAIL:	Hard-boiled rain.
HAIR TONIC:	A pick-me-up medicine for big rabbits.
HERMIT:	A lady's glove.
HIPPIES:	Things your leggies are attached to.
HOGWASH:	A pig's laundry.
HYPOCHON-DRIAC:	A case of sham pain.

I

ICE LOLLY:	What eskimoes use for money.
ICICLE:	An eavesdropper.
IGLOO:	What Igs use when they want to go to the toilet.
ILLEGAL:	A mighty sick bird.

J

JET SETTER:	A flying dog.

K

KINDRED:	A morbid fear of relatives.
KITTIWAKE:	Time for the cat to get up.
KNAPSACK:	An extremely uncomfortable bed.
KNIGHTHOOD:	A funny hat worn by knights.

L

LAP OF HONOUR: To sit on one's lover's knees.

LAZYBONES: An idle skeleton.

LOBSTER: Another name for a tennis player.

LOOFAH: A lavatory in the distance.

M

MAMMOTH: A moth who's a mother.

MERMAID: A deep-she fish.

METRONOME: A dwarf in Paris's subway system.

MINIMUM: A tiny little mother.

MOONBEAMS: Things that hold the moon up.

N

NIGHTINGALE: An extremely windy evening.

O

OCTOPUS: An eight-legged cat.

P

PARACHUTIST:	One of society's drop-outs.
PARAKEET:	A wordy birdie.
PASTEURISE:	Far beyond what you can see.
PEN FRIENDS:	Pigs who get on well together
PLAYPEN:	An instrument used by William Shakespeare.
POLITICS:	A parrot who has swallowed a clock.
POLYFILLA:	Material used to stuff parrots.

R

RELIEF:	What trees do every Spring.
RIDING-CROP:	Horses growing in a field.

S

SCHOOL

SPIRIT:	A ghost in search of an education.
SCRAPBOOK:	A boxer's diary.
SHAMROCK:	A fake diamond.
SHORT-CUT:	A very little wound.
SKIN-DIVER:	A mosquito.
SPELLBOUND:	How a dictionary is covered.
SOLVENT:	Air-conditioning for shoes.
SPRINGTIME:	When you sit on a drawing pin.
SQUARE ROOT:	Diced turnip.
SUCCEED:	What a budgie with no teeth does.
SYNONYM:	A word you use in place of one you can't spell.

T

TEARS:	Glum drops.
TIDDLYWINKS:	A sleeping drunkard.
TOUPEE:	A top secret.
TORNADO:	Nature doing the twist.
TROJAN HORSE:	A phoney pony.

U

UNABRIDGED: A river you have to swim across.

V

VOLCANO: A mountain that blows its top.

W

WHEELER-DEALER: A car tyre salesman.

WITCHCRAFT: A flying broomstick.

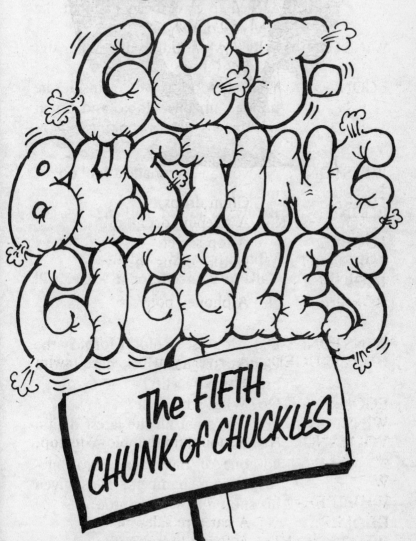

THE REAL GHOSTBUSTERS™

GUT-BUSTING GIGGLES

The FIFTH CHUNK of CHUCKLES

EGON:	I know Peter's always been tactless but this evening when we had to go into that crematorium which was alleged to have been haunted, he really went too far.
WINSTON:	Why – what did he do? What did he say?
EGON:	Well, as soon as we got inside, he jumped up on a table and cried: 'Hi there – what's cooking?'
WINSTON:	No woman ever made a fool out of me.
EGON:	Really. Who did it, then?
EGON:	Whatever I say *goes*!
JANINE:	Talk to yourself for a while, will you?
WINSTON:	Did you see old Morbid the Undertaker has given his place a brand-new facelift?
EGON:	No. What's he done?
WINSTON:	Well, he's got all the latest digital coffins in his window. And he's got one of those new cryogenic-suspension chambers. He's given his shop a new name, too.
EGON:	What is it?
WINSTON:	*'The Departure Lounge'*

EGON: Peter, I'd like you to make some notes about this gang of ghosts we've just busted. Don't forget to detail how many there are, and their revolting habits, and...

PETER: Uh, Egon, where shall I make all these notes?

EGON: You fool! Didn't you bring your exorcise book with you?

JANINE: Egon, what's the best place to look for monster snails?

EGON: At the end of monster's fingers, I suppose.

PETER: I didn't have an education. After only a few days, I got thrown out of Rodean.

RAY: But Rodean is a school for *girls*.

PETER: I know. That's why I was thrown out.

1ST
GHOUL: Why have you tied a great big knot in your neck?

2ND
GHOUL: I've got a bit of a head-cold, and I don't want it to go to my chest.

PETER: I wish I had been born in the Dark Ages.

JANINE: So do I. You look terrible in the light.

On silent tiptoe The Real Ghostbusters moved through the dark sinister house where Wanda the wild witch lived. Noticing a chink of light coming from one room, they went across to it and, with bated breath, listened to the hideous cacklings that came from within: 'I'm going to bite off your arms,' Wanda was screeching. 'Then I'm going to chew off your legs, and then I'm going to bite off your head . . .'

'Okay guys . . . take her!' Egon shouted, kicking down the door. Followed closely by the other Ghostbusters, he crashed into the room to see . . .

Wanda the witch eating a stack of jelly babies.

'Like some, loonies?' she leered.

75

BOY GHOST:	Doris, darling, I'd like to get you a present. Is there anything special you'd like?
GIRL GHOST:	Yes, Percy. I'd love some jewels, made of really special stones.
BOY GHOST:	Sure, sweetheart – any particular kind of stones?
GIRL GHOST:	Yes, Percy. *Tombstones*.

A man in a cinema nearly choked on his drink-on-a-stick when a pale, flickering, phantom-like shape drifted out of the ether and sat down beside him.

MAN:	Excuse me . . . . are you . . . . a ghost?
GHOST:	Yes, that's right.
MAN:	But what . . . . are you . . . . doing . . . . *here*?
GHOST:	Well, actually, I liked the book!

PETER:	You have to be crazy to get by these days.
WINSTON:	Yep. Otherwise, you'd go completely round the bend!

Slimer was lurking in a big store, right alongside the foot of the escalator, peering intently at the moving handrail.

'Can I help you, sir?' asked one the assistants.

'Nope,' said Slimer, with an evil grin. 'I'm just waiting for my chewing-gum to come back. Goop, doop, boop.'

EGON: What became of that girl I saw you with in that hammock?

RAY: Oh, we fell out.

JANINE:	I felt really generous this morning, so I gave a decrepit-looking tramp a pound for a meal.
EGON:	Very kind of you Janine. And what did your boyfriend have to say about that?
JANINE:	Oh, not much. Just 'Thanks'.

Egon, who was giving a scientific discourse on his latest theories to the rest of The Ghostbusters, suspected that they weren't paying very close attention to him. So he decided to lapse into meaningless double-talk to see if they were still awake.

EGON: The other problems relating to paranormal duobatics are of course globnicks, refrominating particles, and the oscillating wagon-wheels of bubonic vegetables. Obviously, although blinger-bleeps can be used to detect the scallopy shells of individual fruit pies, the co-relationship of the grimshanks is predetermined by the spokes of the bicycle shed.

PETER: Yeah, I think we read you on that, Egon. But what on earth are Wagon Wheels?

GHOST
TEACHER: Right, class, has everyone got the hang of making themselves invisible and walking through walls?

GIRL
GHOST: Please, Miss, I'm still not sure how it's done.

GHOST
TEACHER: Very well, Melanie. Now just watch the blackboard and I'll go through it once more . . . .

When off-duty, Winston drives a Datsun car, which he is very pleased with. One day, though, it went 'clunkety-clunk-splaaaat!' and stopped. He couldn't get it started again, so he took it to the garage to be repaired. But he was told that it was a very early model Datsun, and that the special cog that was broken was no longer being made.

'You'll have to have the cog especially built,' said the mechanic. 'And you'll have to buy a minimum of a hundred cogs.'

Since the car wouldn't work without it, Winston reckoned that he would have to buy a hundred of the cogs. So eager was he to get his car started, he flew to Japan and brought the cogs back home with him on his lap.

As the plane neared home, the captain announced that there was slight engine trouble, and ordered all the passengers to jettison any extra weight. With a sigh, Winston slipped one of the cogs into his pocket; and flung the other ninety-nine overboard.

Way down on the ground below, a farm couple were just sitting down to dinner. The wife suddenly looked out of the window and remarked to her husband: 'Why, look, Jethro–it's raining Datsun cogs!'

WINSTON: Do you believe in clubs for ghosts?
EGON: Only if kindness fails.

GRUESOME GUSSIE: I tried to join a Lonely Hearts Club, with the hope of meeting someone who was attractive, rich and would love me for my adorable self.

HOWLING HARRY: What happened?

GRUESOME GUSSIE: They sent back my picture, and said that nobody in their right mind would want to meet me, *however* lonely they were!

RAY: Gosh, this ointment for my shoulder doesn't half make this bruise smart.
PETER: Try rubbing some into your head.

EGON: What shall we have for dinner, Janine?

JANINE: How about those things you first throw away the outside and cook the inside, then you eat the outside and throw away the inside.

EGON: What on earth do you mean?

JANINE: Corn-on-the-cob, of course.

1ST
PHANTOM: Have you read the 'Tibetan Book Of The Dead'?

2ND
PHANTOM: No. I'm waiting for it to come out on video.

FARMER: If you Ghostbusters can't get rid of the phantoms who are haunting my barn, I'm going to have to turn my farm into a café.

RAY: Why's that?

FARMER: Well, the ghosts have spooked my animals . . . . The cows are giving milkshakes and all the chickens are laying scrambled eggs!

WINSTON: I can hear a strange, eerie, spooky, hollow, other-worldly knocking sound.

PETER: So can I.

EGON: So can I.

RAY: Sorry, guys . . . It's my knees.

COULD YOU
BE A

GHOSTBUSTER?

A QUESTIONNAIRE

Some people are born Ghostbusters, some are born idiots, while others are born with a cute little sprinkling of freckles on their noses. (This is rather besides the point, but it's nice to know, isn't it?) The thing is, do you ever pause in your workaday round and think: 'Gee–I'd love to be a Ghostbuster' or even 'I wonder if I am constructed of the stuff that Ghostbusters are?' Should, however, you pause and think 'Shall I play hide-and-seek with my knees today?', then clearly you are not well. Get out of this book immediately and go and have a lie-down somewhere, because you are wasting everybody's time.

So here's your golden chance to find out whether you're Ghostbuster material or not. It takes a very special kind of person to qualify; a person steeped in the very gifts and qualities that heroes are made of. Unlimited courage. Trust. A high intellectual level. A wild and restless sense of adventure. A devotion to truth, honesty and justice. The ability to withstand pain, suffering and deprivation. A keen sense of curiosity. The driving need to explore new frontiers of human experience. Boundless selflessness. Humility. A basic desire to serve one's fellow-man. Bravery. Tenacity. A deep sense of tradition, values and loyalty.

In other words, a right smarmy little prig.

But never mind, it takes all sorts to make a world. And spread before you now is not only the world, but also a questionnaire, to help you find out if you've got what it takes to bust ghosts, win friends and influence politicians.

Just tick the answers by 'a', 'b' or 'c' as you think fit. Then check it out with the scoring chart at the end, and refer to the ratings table. And that's it. Good luck, and good busting!

1. If you unexpectedly met a ghost, would you:
(a) Whimper and faint.
(b) Cry 'God for Harry, England and St George!' and thrash it.
(c) Challenge it to a game of bent Scrabble.

2. How did you spend your last holiday:
(a) Hiding in a cupboard.
(b) Mountaineering.
(c) Sleeping, and plotting revenge against society.

3. Who is your hero out of these?
(a) Doris Day.
(b) Superman.
(c) Roy of the Rovers.

4. An alligator suddenly appears in your bath. What do you say to it?
(a) 'See you later, alligator . . . .'
(b) 'You don't scare me, handbag-features!'
(c) 'Anything on TV tonight?'

5. Would you spend the night alone in a haunted house?
(a) No, no, please don't make me!
(b) Certainly – no bother.
(c) Sure, if I can take my girlfriend along.

6. You witness a thief snatching a poor old lady's handbag. What course of action do you adopt?
(a) Snatch her umbrella.
(b) Pursue the villain and arrest him.
(c) Run – in the opposite direction.

7. What is the motto of the Boy Scouts?
(a) 'Who's For Porridge?'
(b) 'Be Prepared'.
(c) 'Dance To The Jailhouse Rock'.

8. What is the Institute For Psychical Research devoted to?
(a) It's grandmother.
(b) Knowledge of supernatural happenings.
(c) One-man bands.

9. Where do flies go in the winter-time?
(a) Into hiding.
(b) To tropical climes.
(c) Into currant buns.

10. What do you think of this Questionnaire so far?
(a) Not a lot.
(b) Absolutely brilliant.
(c) When I wake up, I'll tell you.

11. What is 'ectoplasm'
(a) A frozen TV dinner.
(b) Vapour exuded by a moving spirit.
(c) A new punk-rock group, with banjoes.

12. What is Egon's profession?
(a) Hairdresser to hamsters.
(b) Ghostbuster.
(c) Worm-trainer.

13. What does the acronym N.A.T.O. stand for?
(a) 'Never Attack The Ostriches.'
(b) 'North Atlantic Treaty Organisation.'
(c) 'Normal Activity Tires me Out.'

14. What is your favourite cake?
(a) A danish pastry.
(b) A doughnut.
(c) Bread pudding.

15. Think back to when you last attacked somebody in anger. Which weapon did you use:
(a) An ironic epigram.
(b) Bare fists.
(c) A chain-saw.

16. Could you disturb a coven of witches and ask
them to darn your socks?
(a) No, I wouldn't dare.
(b) Yes.
(c) I don't wear socks.

17. It's announced that we are at war with Tonga, a tiny island in the Pacific. What is your immediate reaction?
(a) Blind panic.
(b) Enlist, and request action.
(c) Yawn, and carry on playing pool.

18. Ought one to kiss on a first date?
(a) Yes, providing one's alone.
(b) No; kissing saps one's natural aggression.
(c) Only *one* kiss?

19. Of all the qualities needed to be Ghostbuster, which do you think is the most important?
(a) The ability to sprint backwards.
(b) A basic desire to serve one's fellow man.
(c) The energy to fill out questionnaires.

20. How do you think The Ghostbusters are thought of by the general public?
(a) Rather cute.
(b) Brave, upstanding fighting men; a credit to the nation.
(c) Mindless thugs, seeking thrills in violence.

SCORING

For every 'a' you've ticked you get 0 points.

For every 'b' you've ticked you get 10 points.

For every 'c' you've ticked you get 5 points.

For every miniature drawing of the Taj Mahal you've drawn, you get no points, but a special award of a fireman's hat.

For every crude doodle you've done, deduct 5 points from your score and tweak your own nose.

Now add up your score. It should be somewhere between 0 and 200. Have a rest, then proceed to the ratings ceremony . . .

YOUR GHOSTBUSTERS-ABILITY RATING

0–10 points. You're a bit of a twit, aren't you? Are you sure you did the right questionnaire, and with the right end of the pen? If you did do it, and this is your real score, you'd better forget any dreams of glory you ever had. Position yourself in a gutter, and be ready to cheer when the heroes go marching by.

11–50 points. Whether you like it or not, you're a wimp. It's arguable whether you have any brain or not, but for certain you have a yellow rubber spine and can be scared by anyone batting their eyelids close to you. But don't panic; possibly you're in the majority. Who knows? Who cares?

51–100 points: You fall into the pathetic 'Tries Hard' category; sort of a coward with a conscience. Best to blend in with the scenery and not come out till playtime.

101–150 points: You'd made an excellent buddy, a first-rate captain of industry, maybe even a passable offspin bowler for Gloucestershire. But you seem to lack that certain 'Up-and-at-'em-before-they-crush-you' spark in your personality. Try a course of primal therapy (screaming at yourself) and you may well improve.

151–190 points: You are perfect Ghostbuster material. You have all the qualities, and the humility that enables you to use them with elan and panache. Go West, Young Man . . . . Go to Hollywood, and bust.

191–200 points: Gosh, I bet you're a *wow* at parties. You're altogether too brilliant in every department to be real; you lack any sign of compassion or humanity . . . . You don't happen to be a *ghost*, do you?

MORE OF

Janine's

LOOPY

LIMERICKS

Slimer once journeyed to Loch Ness;
Met the Monster, who left him a mess;
They returned his entrails
By the regular mails,
And the rest of the stuff by express.

There's a ghost in the town of West Looe,
Who bites all her victims in two.
She has a misgiving,
Should any be living,
They'd raise such a hullabaloo.

A careless zoo-keeper named Blake,
Fell into a tropical lake;
Said a fat alligator,
A few minutes later:
'Quite nice! Though I much prefer steak.'

An other-worldly youth in Cologne,
With a pain in his stomach did moan;
He heaved a great sigh,
Saying, 'I might as well die;
But the loss would be only my own.'

A morbid young chap from Port Clyde,
In a funeral procession was spied.
When asked 'Who is dead?'
He giggled and said:
'Search me—I'm just here for the ride.'

A talkative fellow named Lister,
Went walking one day with his sister;
A bull at one poke,
Tossed her into an oak,
It was two months before Lister missed her.

Ray, on holiday in Shoreham,
Made paper-tissue trousers and wore 'em:
He looked smart and neat,
Till he bent in the street,
To pick up a coin, then he tore 'em.

A fly and a flea in a flue,
Were imprisoned with nothing to do:
Said the fly, 'Let us flee!'
'Let us fly!' said the flea—
So they flew through the flaw in the flue.

An elegant lady named Psyche,
Was heard to exclaim, 'Oh, crikey!'
For, when riding her bike,
She tripped over a pike,
And fell on some rails that were spiky.

'I wish that my room had a floor,'
Said Winston, in digs on a moor:
'All this walking around,
Without touching the ground,
Is getting to be such a bore.'

A nervous young lady of Weams,
Was troubled with nightmarish dreams;
She would wake in the night,
And, in terrible fright,
Shake the beams of her house with her screams.

There was an old phantom from Clewer,
Whose wife was as thin as a skewer.
Last night, sad to say,
She suddenly passed away,
Through the bars of a drain to the sewer.

Peter, having nothing much to do,
Once dreamed he had turned bright blue.
He sat right up in bed,
Took a look at his head,
And found it was perfectly true!

Egon, whilst on a case in Khartoum,
Kept a real greenhouse in his room.
'It reminds me,' he said,
'Of a friend who is dead,
But I cannot remember just whom.'

A peculiar old lady from Herm,
Tied bows to the tail of a worm.
Saying, 'You look so festive;
Do not become restive;
You'll wriggle them off if you squirm.'

A hippo from the Isle of Biscay,
Decided to take up ballet:
She stood on her toes,
And said 'Well, here goes!'
And with a splash she emptied the bay.

An eccentric old madame of Rhyl,
Wrote a very queer clause in her will;
It read 'To the Mayor,
I bequeath my false hair;
There's enough a nice cushion to fill.'

In the midst of an anthem of Grace,
Slimer quietly slipped from his place,
For a quick game of tag,
With an elderly hag,
Then returned with a smile on his face.

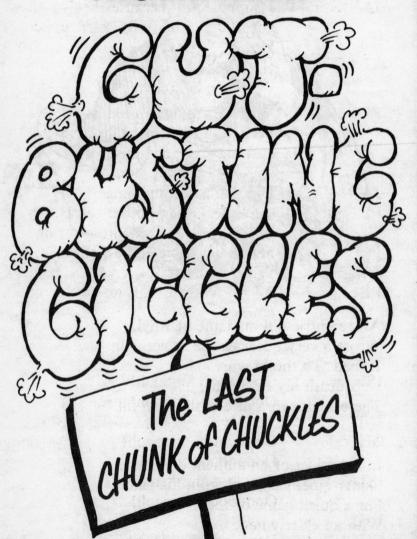

RAY: Why are Englishmen so dreadful
            when it comes to using a hula-
            hoop?
JANINE: I suppose it's because they've all
            got those frightfully stiff upper
            hips.

PETER: Whew, I'm exhausted. I've just
            been with the other Ghostbusters,
            clearing out a house with evil
            spirits in it.
JANINE: Did you catch anything?
PETER: Yep . . . . Got seventeen ghosts, ten
            fiends, seven phantoms, one
            headless zombie and a keefer.
JANINE: What's a keefer?
PETER: To lock them all up with, of
            course!

1ST GHOST: Ooooooooooooooh!
           Ooooooooooooooh!
2ND
GHOST: Ooooooooooooooh!
           Ooooooooooooooh!
1ST GHOST: Oooooooooh! Arrrgh!
           Ooooooooooooooh!
2ND
GHOST: Don't change the subject.

Winston and Ray were crossing a busy street when suddenly a motor-bike zoomed by and ran over Ray's foot. He gave a yelp of pain and collapsed onto the ground.

'Don't just stand there!' Ray cried to Winston. 'Call me an ambulance!'

'Okay, if it'll make you feel better,' shrugged Winston. 'You're an ambulance.'

1ST GHOUL:	What's that book you're reading?
2ND GHOUL:	I think it's a cook book; it's called 'How to Serve Your Fellowman.'

RAY:	See that old house over there? We caught a ghost in it who was haunting the inhabitants in the shape of a giant turnip.
GIRL:	Gosh. And are there any other spooky stories connected with the place?
RAY:	No. It's a one-storey building.

EGON:	Are you sure all the ghosts we captured are lying perfectly flat?
PETER:	Sure, Egon. I used a spirit-level.
PETER:	If I saw somebody being cruel to a monkey, and I stopped them, what would I be showing?
JANINE:	Brotherly love.
EGON:	Now, Sir, I'd like you to describe the fiend you saw flitting across the moor last night.
LOCAL:	Well, he was green, about eleven foot tall, and had purple smoke coming out of his head.
EGON:	Yes, go on.
LOCAL:	And he was bouncing along on a cloud of weird-smelling vapour, reaching over fifty foot high in places.
EGON:	Yes, carry on.
LOCAL:	Oh, and he was chanting something in Latin, and when he did this, the trees in front of him exploded. And a bright glowing orange mushroom kept popping out of his head and then popping back in again.
EGON:	I see, Sir. But did you notice anything *unusual* about him?

PETER:	That's Life.
RAY:	What's Life?
PETER:	A magazine.
RAY:	How much does it cost?
PETER:	Two-ninety five.
RAY:	I've only got two-fifty five.
PETER:	That's Life.
RAY:	What's Life?
PETER:	A magazine . . .

PETER:	Hey, Janine, did you hear the one about the eight friendish ghosts?
JANINE:	No. So tell me.
PETER:	Well, they were called Do, Re, Fa, So, La, Ti and Do.
JANINE:	What about Mi?
PETER:	Sorry, I forgot about you!

JANINE: I now have a new hobby; keeping goldfish as pets.

RAY: Where do you keep them?

JANINE: In the bath-tub.

RAY: But what do you do when you want to have a bath?

JANINE: I blindfold them, silly!

PETER: When did you first suspect there was a ghost hiding under your bed, ma'am?

WOMAN: The morning I woke up with my nose squashed against the ceiling.

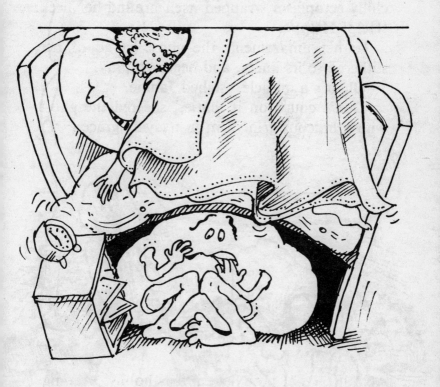

GHOUL: I'd like seven yards of turquoise satan for my wife.

ASSISTANT: I presume you mean *satin*, sir. Satan is something that looks like the devil.

GHOUL: I didn't know you'd met my wife!

'I'm going to eat you all up and spit out your bones,' a ghost suddenly shrieked to Janine, who had been daft enough to take a short-cut home through a haunted car park.

'Help me, O Lord!' Janine cried, as the ghost's chilly ectoplasm wrapped itself around her neck. 'Help! Help!'

To her amazement, the ghost let go of her, slithered to its knees, and began to pray.

'Oh–it's a miracle,' sighed Janine.

'Don't count on it, cutie,' sneered the ghost, with a hideous grin. 'I'm just saying grace . . .'

WINSTON:	There's a witch who lives by the sea.
EGON:	So what?
WINSTON:	She's too scared to go in the sea.
EGON:	So?
WINSTON:	Guess what they call her?
EGON:	I don't know. What?
WINSTON:	Chicken Sandwitch.

| 1ST GHOST: | I don't feel very well. |
| 2ND GHOST: | Just take it easy. I'll go and call a surgical spirit. |

GHOSTBUS-TERS:	Well, Jonathan, that's another dazzling, rib-tickling work of art you've created.
JONA-THAN:	Yep. Guess it is.
GHOST-BUSTERS:	We sure are proud of you; upholding the fine traditions of English humour; projecting trenchant satire, laced with a bright poetic thread of sophisticated wit.
JONA-THAN:	Aw, shucks, it was nothing.
GHOST-BUSTERS:	Oh, there's one thing we've always wondered about, Jonathan; do you like being a writer?
JONA-THAN:	It's not too bad. I just hate the *paperwork*!